Rose

Tulips

Orchids

Sunflower

Lilies

Daffodils

Marigold

Lotus

Dahlia

Gladioli

Carnations

Chrysanthemum

Apple Blossom

Atlantic Puffin

Iris

Lilac

Peonies

Sweet Pea

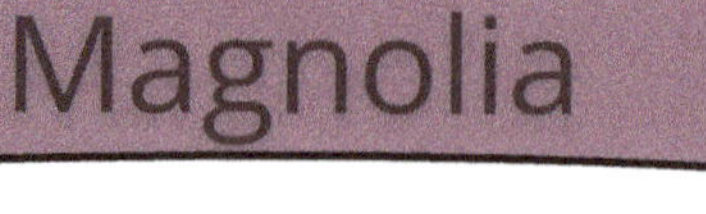

Magnolia

Lavender

Hydrangea

Stock

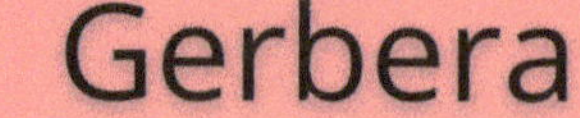

Gerbera

Proteas

Poinsettia

Snapdragons

Lisianthus

Freesia

Plumeria

Queen Anne's Lace

Delphinium

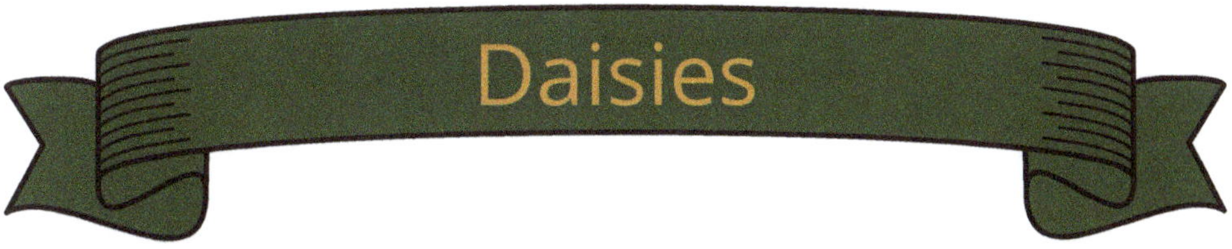

Daisies

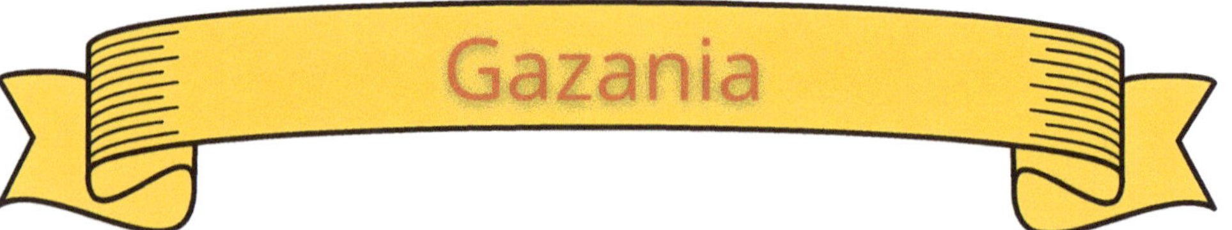

Gazania

Bird of Paradise

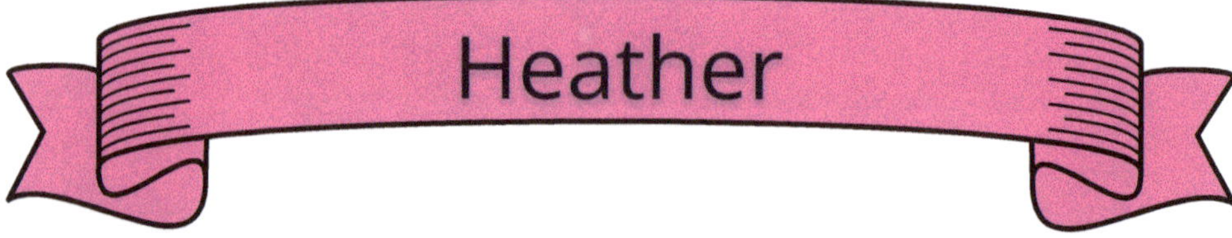

Heather

Anthurium

Anemone

Crocus

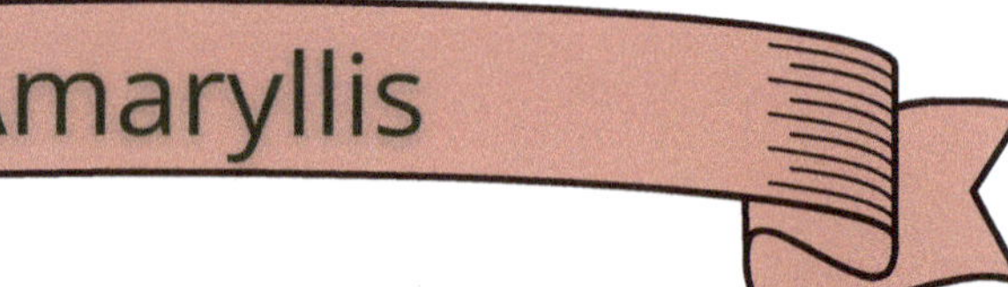

Amaryllis

Pansy

Alstromeria

Clivia

Cherry Blossom

English Daisy

Fairy Wren

Jasmine

Chocolate Cosmos

Morning Glory

Snow Goose

Begonia

Jade Vine

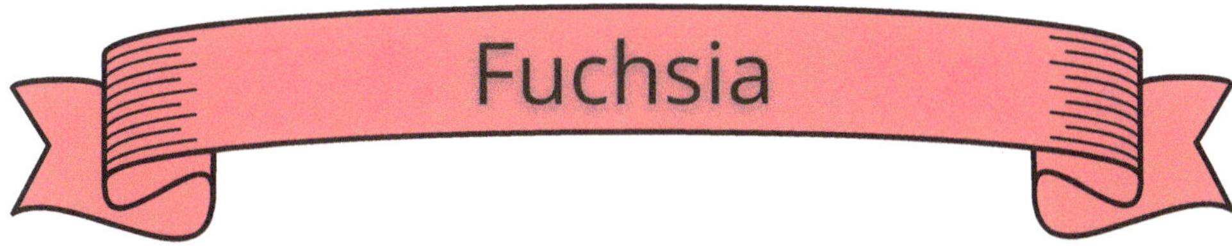

Fuchsia

Bellflower

Parrot's Beak

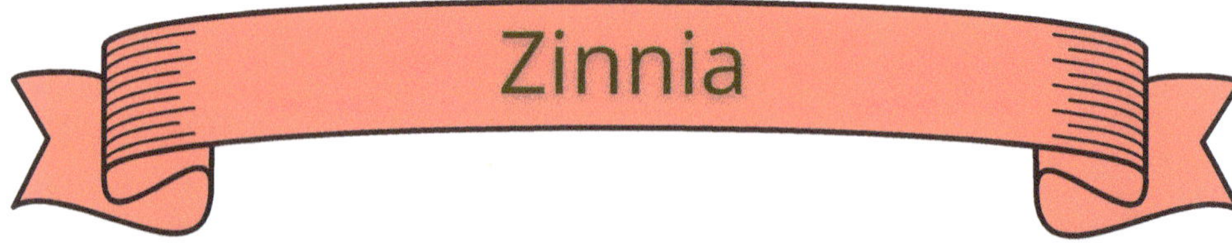
Zinnia

Passion Flower

Columbine

Bleeding Heart

Azalea

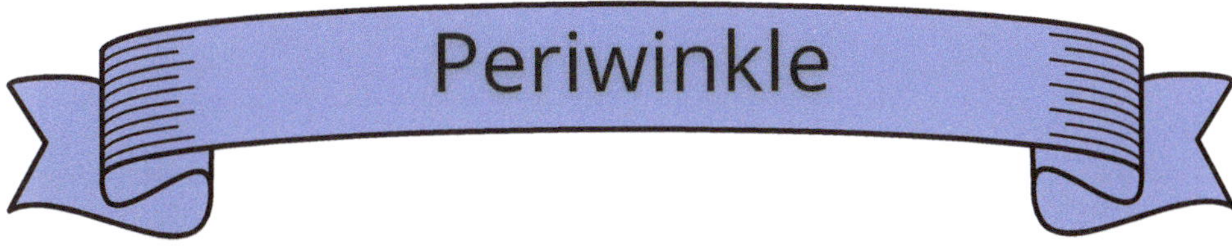

Periwinkle